United States
Department of
Agriculture

Forest Service

Southern
Research Station

Resource Bulletin
SRS–183

Arkansas' Timber Industry— An Assessment of Timber Product Output and Use, 2009

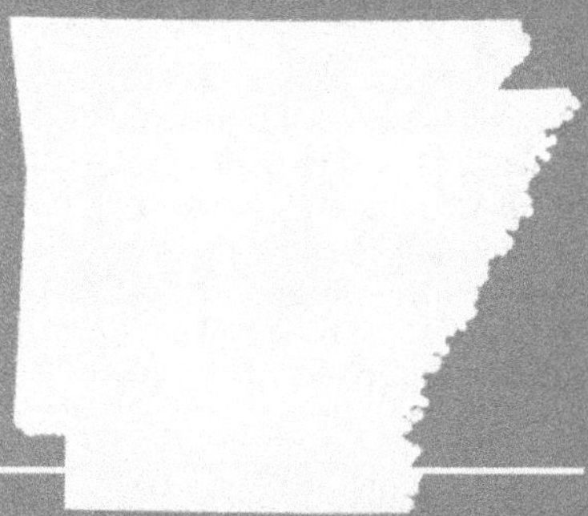

Consuelo Brandeis,
Tony G. Johnson,
Michael Howell, and
James W. Bentley

The Authors:

Consuelo Brandeis, Forester, U.S. Forest Service,
Southern Research Station, Knoxville, TN 37919;
Tony G. Johnson, Forester, U.S. Forest Service,
Southern Research Station, Asheville, NC 28804;
Michael Howell, Forester, and **James W. Bentley**,
Forester, U.S. Forest Service, Southern Research
Station, Knoxville, TN 37919.

September 2011

Southern Research Station
200 W.T. Weaver Blvd.
Asheville, NC 28804

Foreword

This report contains the findings of a 2009 canvass of primary wood-using plants in Arkansas, and presents changes in product output and residue use since 2007. It complements the Forest Inventory and Analysis annual inventory of volume and removals from the State's timberland. The canvass was conducted to determine the amount and source of wood receipts and annual timber product drain, by county, in 2009 and to determine interstate and cross-regional movement of industrial roundwood. Only primary wood-using mills were canvassed. Primary mills are those that process roundwood in log or bolt form or as chipped roundwood. Examples of industrial roundwood products are saw logs, pulpwood, veneer logs, poles, and logs used for composite board products. Mills producing products from residues generated at primary and secondary processors were not canvassed. Trees chipped in the woods were included in the estimate of timber drain only if they were delivered to a primary domestic manufacturer.

A canvass of wood processors in Arkansas was conducted in 2010 to obtain information for 2009. In addition, roundwood from out-of-State mills known to be using logs or bolts harvested from Arkansas timberland was incorporated into Arkansas production estimates. Each mill was canvassed by mail or through personal contact at plant locations. Telephone contacts followed mailed questionnaire responses when additional information or clarification of a response was necessary. In the event of a nonresponse, data collected in previous surveys were updated using current data collected for mills of similar size, product type, and location. Surveys for all timber products other than pulpwood began in 1948, and are currently conducted every 2 years.

Pulpwood production data were taken from an annual canvass of all southern pulpmills. Medium density fiberboard, insulating board, and hardboard plants were included in this survey.

Acknowledgments

The authors thank Joanne Lenahan and Robert Fry for review and comments; Carolyn Steppleton and Michael Howell for their tireless efforts in processing and accuracy of the data; Helen Beresford for timber product output database maintenance and support; Anne Jenkins, Janet Griffin, Sharon Johnson, and Charlene Walker for tables, graphs, statistical checking, and styling; and the Southern Research Station (SRS) Technical Publications Team for editorial review and publication of this report.

The SRS gratefully acknowledges the cooperation and assistance provided by the Arkansas Forestry Commission in collecting mill data. Appreciation is also extended to forest industry and mill managers for providing timber products information.

Timber Product Output Database Retrieval System

The Forest Inventory and Analysis (FIA) Research Work Unit of the USDA Forest Service developed the Timber Product Output (TPO) Database Retrieval System to help customers answer questions about timber harvesting and use in the Southern Region. This system acts as an interface to a standard set of consistently coded TPO data for each State and county in the region and Nation. This regional and national set of TPO data consists of 11 variables that describe for each county the roundwood products harvested, logging residues left in the woods, other timber removals (i.e. land clearing and reserved timber removals), and wood and bark residues generated by the county's primary wood-using mills. The system is available through the FIA Web site: http://srsfia2.fs.fed.us/.

The database is well documented and easy to use. The retrieval system allows the user to select the TPO variables of interest and generate a standard set of timber products, removals, and mill residue tables for the specified resource area, State, or region. The system has been logically divided into two sections to assist the user in making specific data requests. In section 1, the user is asked to define the resource area, and section 2 generates tables for the specified area. In each section, the user is asked to supply specific options that will serve to customize the database retrieval.

There are four options available for defining the geographic area of interest. Each option provides an increasing level of detail. The region, subregion, State, or county defines an area. The user selects the option that best suits the level of detail required. Users who select county as an option should be aware that some counties have been combined due to data sensitivity. These combined counties are identified with asterisks in the output tables.

The TPO contacts are listed for each region to provide additional explanation or clarification.

Tony Johnson
Southern Research Station
USDA Forest Service
200 W.T. Weaver Blvd.
Asheville, NC 28804
tjohnson09@fs.fed.us
828-257-4888

Helen Beresford
Southern Research Station
USDA Forest Service
4700 Old Kingston Pike
Knoxville, TN 37919
hberesford@fs.fed.us
865-862-2091

James Bentley
Southern Research Station
USDA Forest Service
4700 Old Kingston Pike
Knoxville, TN 37919
jbentley@fs.fed.us
865-862-2056

Carolyn Steppleton
Southern Research Station
USDA Forest Service
200 W.T. Weaver Blvd.
Asheville, NC 28804
csteppleton@fs.fed.us
828-257-4848

Contents

[a] All tables in this report are available in Microsoft® Excel workbook files. Upon request, these files will be supplied in the format the customer requests.

The use of trade or firm names in this publication is for reader information and does not imply endorsement by the U.S. Department of Agriculture of any product or service.

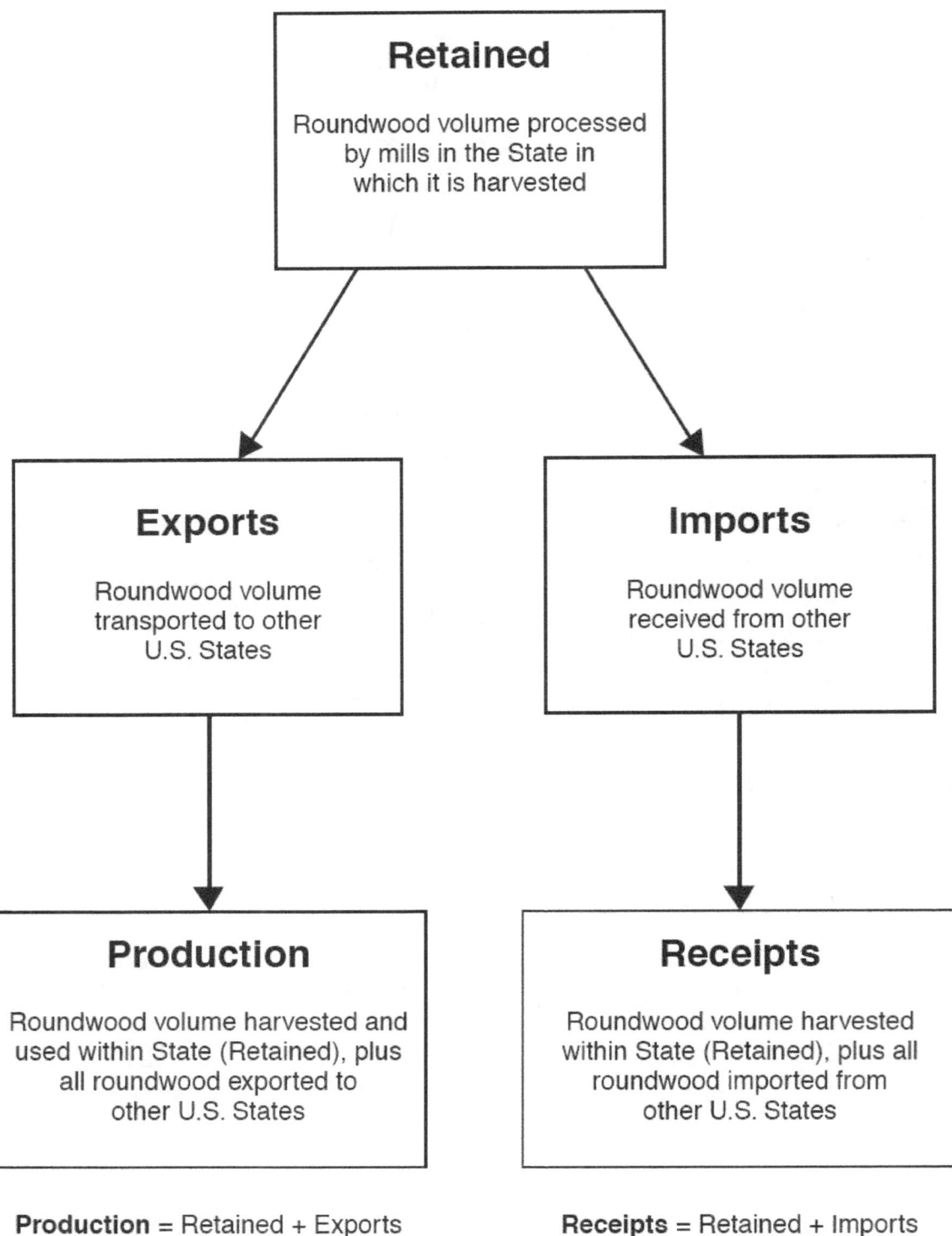

Figure 1—Movement of roundwood exports and imports within the United States.

Arkansas' Timber Industry— An Assessment of Timber Product Output and Use, 2009

Consuelo Brandeis, Tony G. Johnson, Michael Howell, and James W. Bentley

Output of Industrial Timber Products

Note: Certain terms used in this report—retained, export, import, production, and receipts—have specialized meanings and relationships unique to the Forest Inventory and Analysis Units across the country that deal with timber product output (TPO) (fig. 1). Unless otherwise indicated, the context for production and receipts comparisons (increases, decreases, or stabilizations) throughout the report is the change from 2007 to 2009.

All Products

- Arkansas' industrial TPO from roundwood was down 180.3 million cubic feet, or 27 percent, to 489.4 million cubic feet.

- Output of softwood roundwood products declined 24 percent to 361.7 million cubic feet. Similarly, output of hardwood roundwood products fell 35 percent to 127.7 million cubic feet (fig. 2).

- Saw logs and pulpwood were the two main roundwood products in 2009. Together, these two products totaled 429.7 million cubic feet and accounted for 88 percent of the State's total roundwood output (fig. 3).

- Total receipts at Arkansas mills, which included roundwood harvested and retained in the State and roundwood imported from other States, were down 25 percent to 547.5 million cubic feet. Likewise, output of utilized plant byproducts fell 103.2 million cubic feet, or 34 percent, to 196.5 million cubic feet.

- The number of primary roundwood-using plants in Arkansas was down from 141 mills in 2007 to 90 mills in 2009 (fig. 4).

- Across all products, 90 percent of the roundwood harvested was retained for processing at Arkansas mills. Exports of roundwood to other States amounted to 49.3 million cubic feet. Imports of roundwood amounted to 107.4 million cubic feet making the State a net importer of roundwood. Tables A.8 to A.11 show exports to and imports from other States by individual product type.

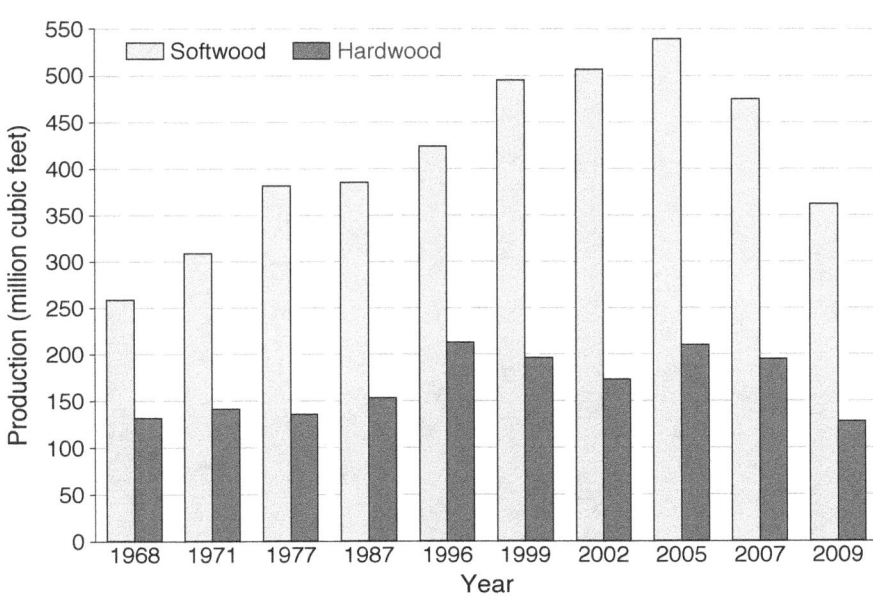

Figure 2—Roundwood production for all products by species group and year (see page 8 for references for individual years), Arkansas.

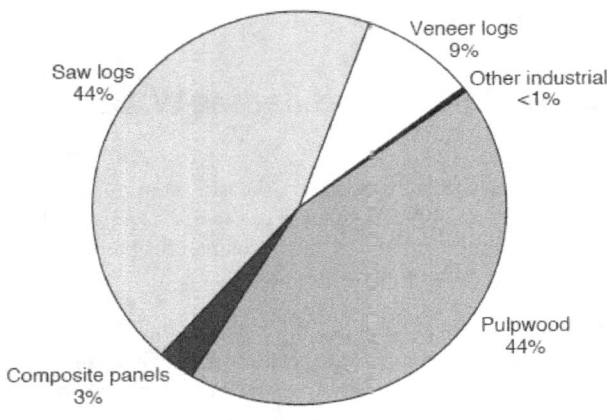

Figure 3—Roundwood production by type of product, Arkansas, 2009.

Saw Logs

- At 215.2 million cubic feet, saw logs accounted for 44 percent of the State's total roundwood products. Output of softwood saw logs fell by 34 percent to 169.8 million cubic feet (943.2 million board feet, International ¼-inch rule). Likewise, output of hardwood saw logs went down 53 percent to 45.5 million cubic feet (274.0 million board feet, International ¼-inch rule) (fig. 5).

- Seventy-five sawmills operated in Arkansas during 2009, a loss of 52 sawmills since 2007. Total saw-log receipts declined 157.4 million cubic feet to 231.2 million cubic feet. Softwood saw-log receipts dropped 36 percent to 188.2 million cubic feet. Hardwood saw-log receipts fell 55 percent to 43.0 million cubic feet.

- Of the 75 sawmills operating in 2009, 71 percent had receipts < 10 million board feet, while 29 percent (22 mills) had receipts of ≥ 10 million board feet. Those 22 mills accounted for 86 percent of total saw-log receipts.

- Arkansas retained 96 percent of its saw-log production for in-State manufacture. Saw-log imports amounted to 24.2 million cubic feet, while exports totaled 8.2 million cubic feet, making the State a net importer of saw logs.

Pulpwood

- Total pulpwood production, including chipped round-wood, dropped 7 percent to 214.5 million cubic feet (2.9 million cords), and accounted for 44 percent of the State's total roundwood TPO. Softwood pulpwood output fell 2 percent to 133.2 million cubic feet (1.84 million cords), while hardwood pulpwood output went down 14 percent to 81.3 million cubic feet (1.06 million cords) (fig. 6).

Primary wood-using mills

- • Sawmill (0–5 mmbf)
- ● Sawmill (5–20 mmbf)
- ⬤ Sawmill (>20 mmbf)
- ▲ Composite panel
- ✚ Veneer
- ■ Pulpmill
- ◆ Plywood
- ☆ Other mill

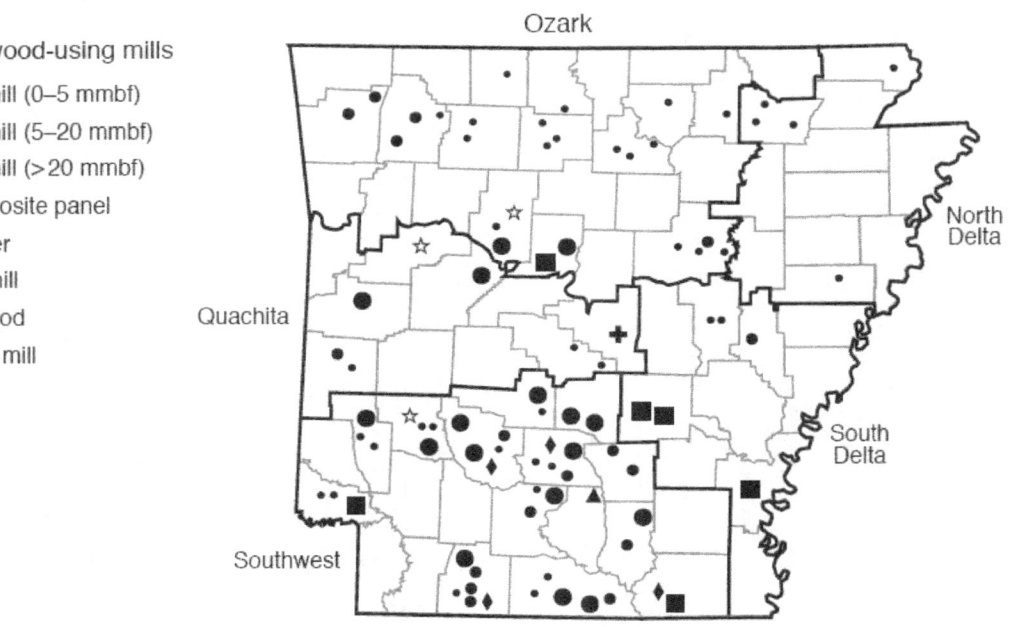

Figure 4—Primary wood-using mills by region, Arkansas, 2009.

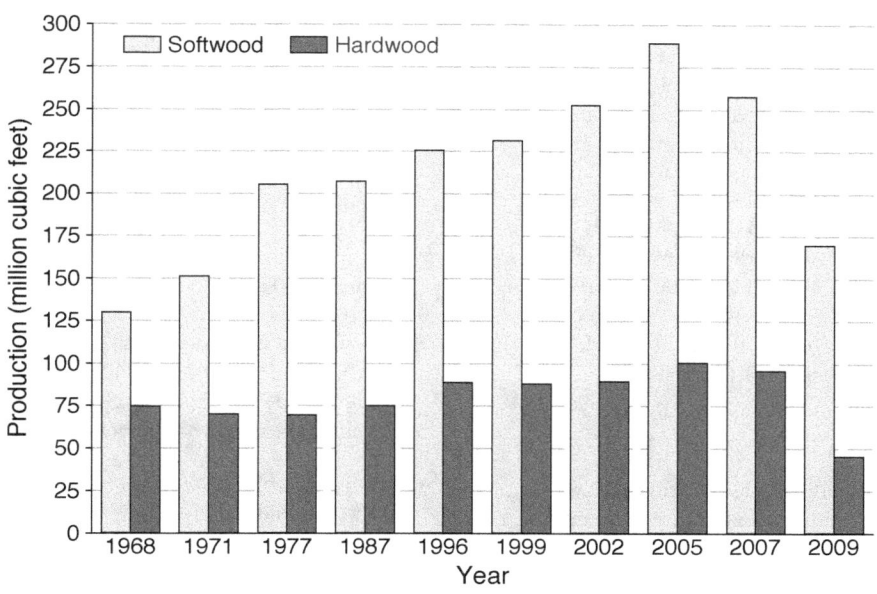

Figure 5—Roundwood saw-log production by species group and year (see page 8 for references for individual years), Arkansas.

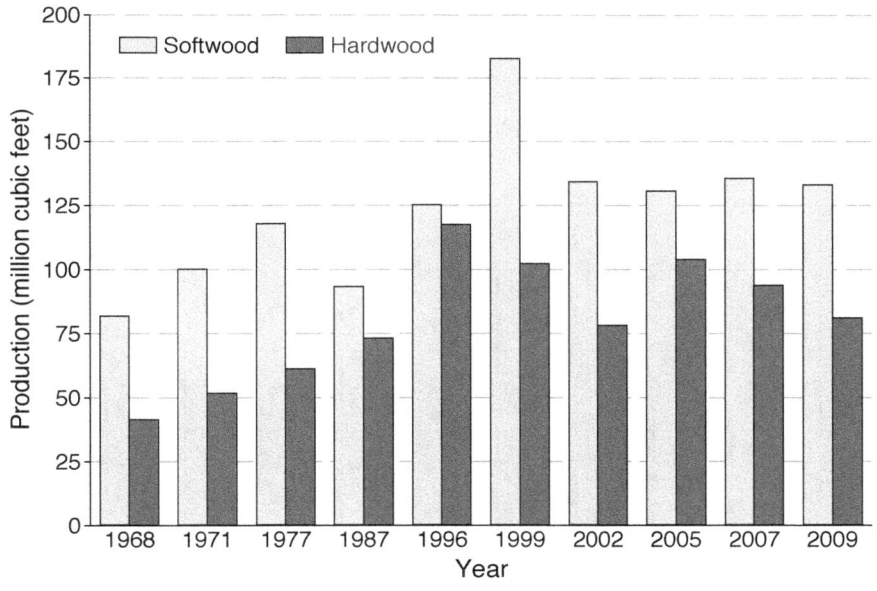

Figure 6—Roundwood pulpwood production by species group and year (see page 8 for references for individual years), Arkansas.

- Six pulpmills were operating and receiving roundwood in 2009, same as in 2007. Total pulpwood receipts for these mills increased 6.6 million cubic feet, or 3 percent, to 248.6 million cubic feet. Pulpwood receipts accounted for 45 percent of total receipts for all mills.

- Eighty-one percent of roundwood cut for pulpwood was retained for processing at Arkansas pulpmills. Roundwood pulpwood accounted for 81 percent of total known exports and 69 percent of total imports. Roundwood pulpwood exports were 40.1 million cubic feet, while imports totaled 74.1 million cubic feet, making the State a net importer of pulpwood.

Veneer Logs

- Output of veneer logs decreased 28 percent to 44.3 million cubic feet, and accounted for 9 percent of the State's total roundwood TPO volume. Softwood veneer production went down 23 percent to 43.3 million cubic feet (249.1 million board feet, International ¼-inch rule). Output of hardwood veneer logs fell 82 percent to 951,000 cubic feet (6.0 million board feet, International ¼-inch rule) (fig. 7).

- Five veneer and plywood mills operated in Arkansas in 2009, a loss of two mills since 2007. Receipts of veneer logs declined 29 percent to 53.3 million cubic feet. Softwood veneer receipts dropped 24 percent to

52.4 million cubic feet. Similarly, hardwood veneer receipts fell 86 percent to 951,000 cubic feet.

- Arkansas retained all of its veneer-log production for processing at in-State veneer mills. With no export volume and imports of 9.0 million cubic feet this makes the State a net importer of roundwood veneer logs during 2009.

Composite Panels

- Roundwood harvested from Arkansas' forest for composite panels dropped 42 percent to 14.3 million cubic feet (196,515 cords). Softwood output accounted for all of the composite panel production (fig. 8).

- Volume of composite panel receipts has been combined with other industrial volume for confidentiality reasons.

Other Industrial Products

- Roundwood harvested for other industrial uses such as poles, posts, firewood, logs for log homes, and other industrial products, increased from 333,000 cubic feet to 1.2 million cubic feet. Softwood accounted for all of the other industrial product output.

- Receipts for other industrial volume, which include composite panel volume, totaled 14.4 million cubic feet.

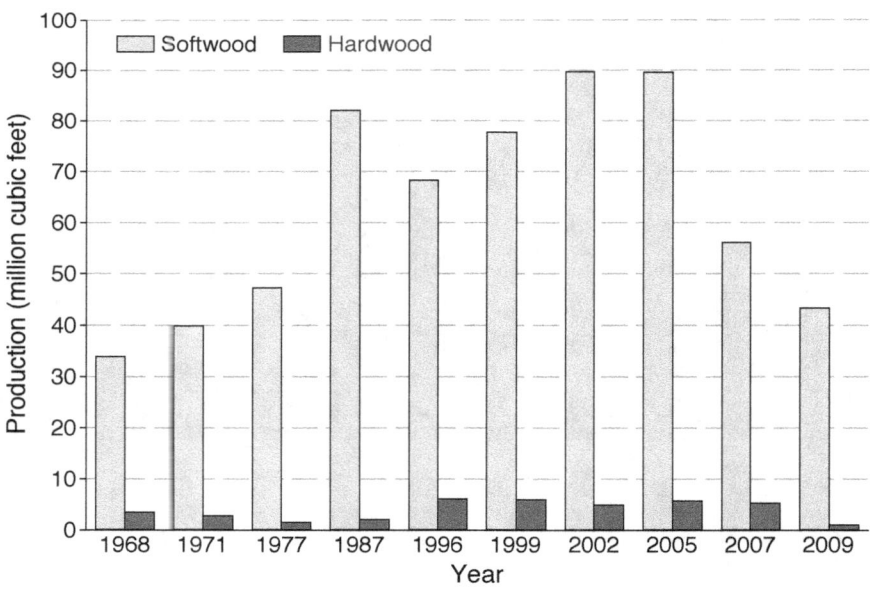

Figure 7—Roundwood veneer-log production by species group and year (see page 8 for references for individual years) Arkansas.

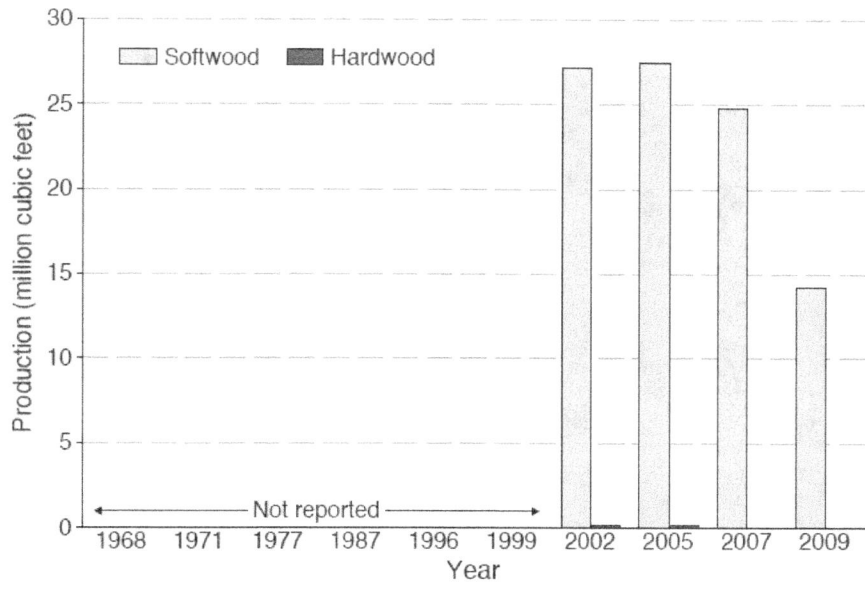

Figure 8—Roundwood production for composite panels by species group and year (see page 8 for references for individual years), Arkansas.

Plant Byproducts

- Processing of primary products in Arkansas mills generated 196.7 million cubic feet of wood and bark residues. Coarse residues from all primary products amounted to 79.8 million cubic feet, while bark volume totaled 51.0 million cubic feet. Together, sawdust and shavings made-up 33 percent of total residues, or 65.9 million cubic feet (fig. 9).

- The processing of saw logs generated 144.9 million cubic feet of residue, 74 percent of the total residues produced (fig. 10).

- Virtually all 196.7 million cubic feet of the wood and bark residues were used for a product. Fifty-six percent of the residues were used for industrial fuel and 37 percent were used for fiber products (fig. 11). About 73.3 million cubic feet, or 92 percent, of the coarse residues were used for fiber products. Most of the bark was used as industrial fuel and miscellaneous products. Eighty-eight percent of the sawdust and shavings was used for industrial fuel.

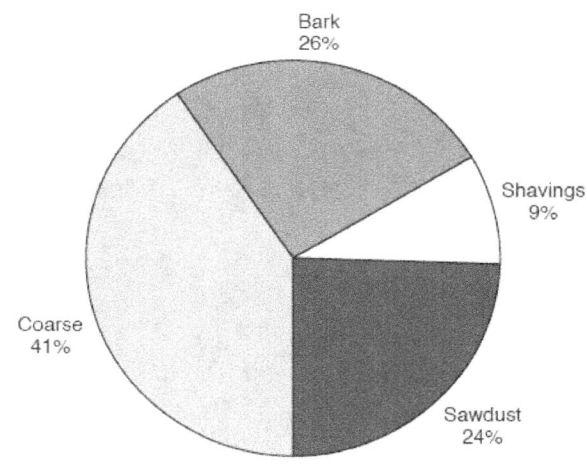

Figure 9—Primary mill residue by residue type, Arkansas, 2009.

5

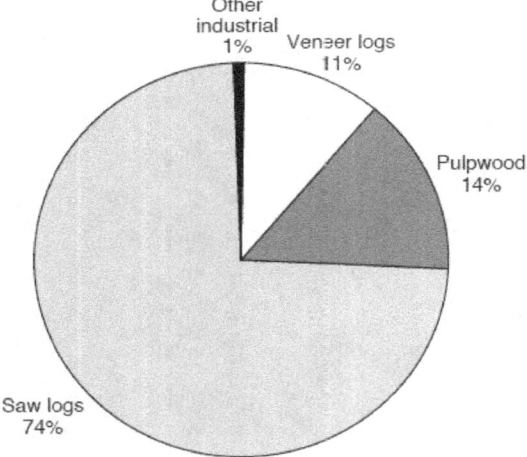

Figure 10—Primary mill residue produced by roundwood type, Arkansas, 2009.

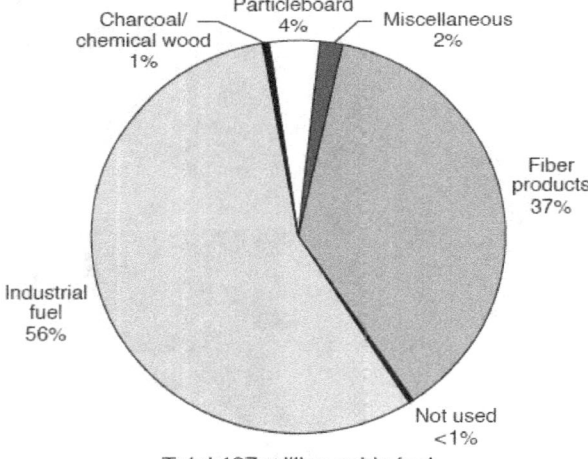

Total 197 million cubic feet

Figure 11—Disposal of residue by product, Arkansas, 2009.

County Data

- Table A.14 shows softwood and hardwood product output by county and individual product type. All 75 counties in Arkansas had roundwood output. Eight counties (Ashley, Bradley, Clark, Cleveland, Dallas, Drew, Pike, and Union) had combined softwood and hardwood product output exceeding 20 million cubic feet each. Together, these eight counties accounted for 204.3 million cubic feet, or 42 percent of the State's total product output.

Total Roundwood Output

The following sections provide product output by source, ownership, and detailed species group, estimated using the most recent inventory data for Arkansas.

Source

- In addition to the 489.4 million cubic feet of roundwood output for industrial roundwood, an estimated 25.3 million cubic feet were harvested for residential fuelwood, bringing Arkansas' total roundwood output to 514.7 million cubic feet.

- Ninety-five percent of total roundwood output was considered growing-stock volume (sawtimber and poletimber) from timberland sources. Other sources (such as saplings; stumps, tops, and limbs of trees on timberland; and trees on nonforest land) contributed an estimated 25.4 million cubic feet, or 5 percent of total roundwood output (fig. 12).

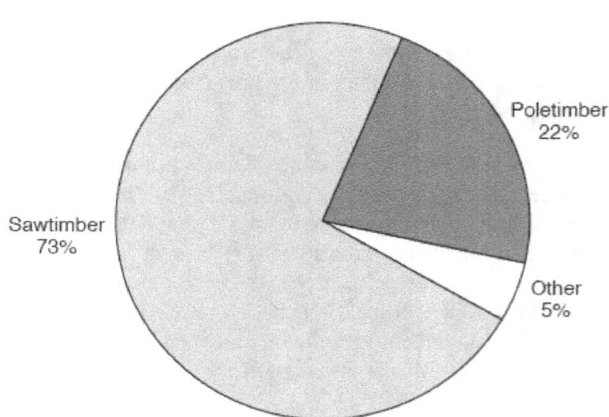

Total 515 million cubic feet

Figure 12—Roundwood output by source, Arkansas, 2009.

Ownership

- Nonindustrial private forest lands contributed 241.4 million cubic feet, or 47 percent, of the total roundwood output. Forest industry lands accounted for 237.2 million cubic feet, or 46 percent of the total output. Public lands made-up the remaining 7 percent, or 36.1 million cubic feet (fig. 13).

Species

- The loblolly and shortleaf pine group provided the most volume of any softwood species group, accounting for 98 percent of the total softwood output. Cedar and cypress accounted for nearly 2 percent, while other yellow pines type provided a marginal volume—under 1 percent (fig. 14). For hardwoods, the red oak and white oak groups combined accounted for 87.8 million cubic feet, or 58 percent of total hardwood output (fig. 15).

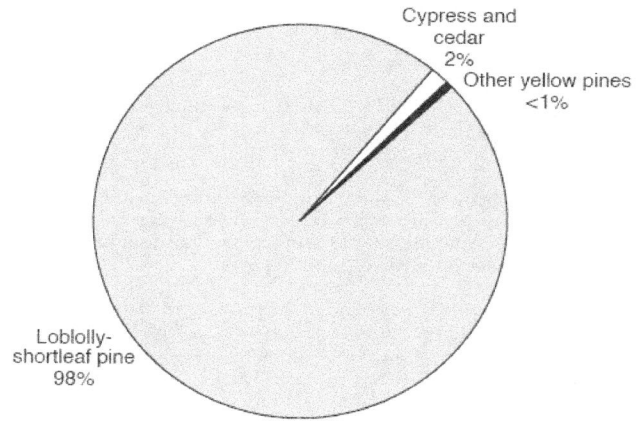

Total 365 million cubic feet

Figure 14—Roundwood output by softwood species group, Arkansas, 2009.

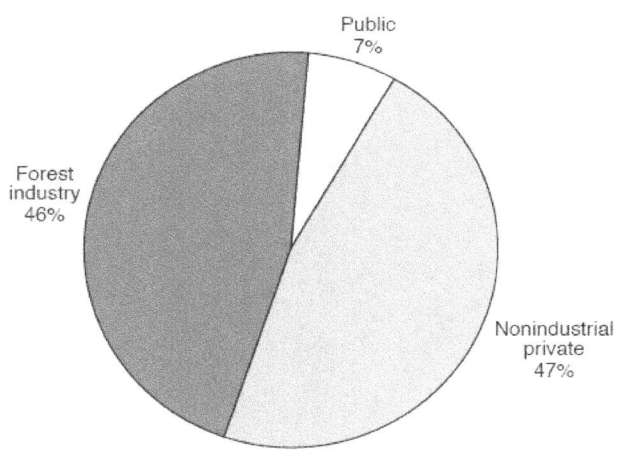

Total 515 million cubic feet

Figure 13—Roundwood output by ownership, Arkansas, 2009.

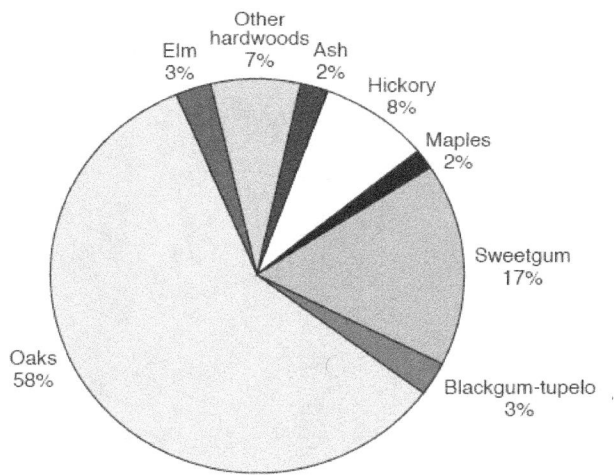

Total 150 million cubic feet

Figure 15—Roundwood output by hardwood species group, Arkansas, 2009.

References

Beltz, R.C. 1970. Arkansas forest industries. Resour. Bull. SO–21. New Orleans: U.S. Department of Agriculture Forest Service, Southern Forest Experiment Station. 28 p. [1968].

Bentley, J.W.; Howell, M.; Johnson, T.G. 2008. Arkansas' timber industry—an assessment of timber product output and use, 2005. Resour. Bull. SRS–132. Asheville, NC: U.S. Department of Agriculture Forest Service, Southern Research Station. 31 p. [2005].

Bentley, J.W.; Howell, M.; Johnson, T.G. 2005. Arkansas' timber industry—an assessment of timber product output and use, 2002. Resour. Bull. SRS–99. Asheville, NC: U.S. Department of Agriculture Forest Service, Southern Research Station. 43 p. [2002].

Bentley, J.W.; Howell, M.; Johnson, T.G. 2002. Arkansas' timber industry—an assessment of timber product output and use, 1999. Resour. Bull. SRS–79. Asheville, NC: U.S. Department of Agriculture Forest Service, Southern Research Station. 40 p. [1999].

Bertleson, D.F. 1973. Arkansas forest industries, 1971. Resour. Bull. SO–38. New Orleans: U.S. Department of Agriculture Forest Service, Southern Forest Experiment Station. 29 p. [1971].

Bertleson, D.F. 1980. Arkansas forest industries, 1977. Resour. Bull. SO–75. New Orleans: U.S. Department of Agriculture Forest Service, Southern Forest Experiment Station. 18 p. [1977].

Howell, M.; Johnson, T.G. 2009. Arkansas' timber industry—an assessment of timber product output and use, 2007. Unpublished report. Asheville, NC: U.S. Department of Agriculture Forest Service, Southern Research Station. 31 p. [2007].

Howell, M.; Levins, R. 1998. Arkansas' timber industry—an assessment of timber product output and use, 1996. Resour. Bull. SRS–28. Asheville, NC: U.S. Department of Agriculture Forest Service, Southern Research Station. 23 p. [1996].

Little, E.L., Jr. 1979. Checklist of United States trees (native and naturalized). Agric. Handb. 541. Washington, DC: U.S. Department of Agriculture. 375 p.

May, D.M. 1990. Development and status of Arkansas' primary forest products industry. Resour. Bull. SO–152. New Orleans: U.S. Department of Agriculture Forest Service, Southern Forest Experiment Station. 28 p. [1987].

Glossary

Board foot. A unit of measure applied to lumber that is 1-foot long, 1-foot wide, and 1-inch thick (or its equivalent) and also associated with roundwood as to its potential yield of such products.

Byproducts. Primary wood products, e.g., pulp chips, animal bedding, and fuelwood, recycled from mill residues.

Composite panels. Roundwood products manufactured into chips, wafers, strands, flakes, shavings, or sawdust and then reconstituted into a variety of panel and engineered lumber products.

Consumption. The quantity of a commodity, such as pulpwood, utilized by a particular mill or group of mills.

Drain. The volume of roundwood removed from any geographic area where timber is grown.

Exports. The volume of domestic roundwood utilized by mills outside the State where timber was cut.

Fiber products. Byproducts used in the manufacture of pulp, paper, paperboard, and composite products, such as chipboard.

Growing-stock removals. The growing-stock volume removed from poletimber and sawtimber trees in the timberland inventory. (Note: Includes volume removed for roundwood products, logging residues, and other removals.)

Growing-stock trees. Living trees of commercial species classified as sawtimber, poletimber, saplings, and seedlings. Growing-stock trees must contain at least one 12-foot or two 8-foot logs in the saw-log portion, currently or potentially (if too small to qualify). The log(s) must meet dimension and merchantability standards and have, currently or potentially, one-third of the gross board-foot volume in sound wood.

Growing-stock volume. The cubic-foot volume of sound wood in growing-stock trees at least 5.0 inches d.b.h. from a 1-foot stump to a minimum 4.0-inch top d.o.b. of the central stem.

Hardwoods. Dicotyledonous trees, usually broadleaf and deciduous.

Soft hardwoods. Hardwood species with an average specific gravity of ≤0.50, such as gums, yellow-poplar, cottonwoods, red maple, basswoods, and willows.

Hard hardwoods. Hardwood species with an average specific gravity >0.50, such as oaks, hard maples, hickories, and beech.

Imports. The volume of domestic roundwood delivered to a mill or group of mills in a specific State but harvested outside that State.

Industrial fuelwood. A roundwood product, with or without bark, used to generate energy at a manufacturing facility such as a wood-using mill.

Industrial roundwood products. Any primary use of the main stem of a tree, such as saw logs, pulpwood, veneer logs, intended to be processed into primary wood products such as lumber, wood pulp, sheathing, at primary wood-using mills.

International ¼-inch rule. A log rule or formula for estimating the board-foot volume of logs, allowing ½-inch of taper for each 4-foot length. The rule appears in a number of forms that allow for kerf. In the form used by FIA, a ¼-inch of kerf is assumed. This rule is used as the U.S. Forest Service standard log rule in the Eastern United States.

Log. A primary forest product harvested in long, primarily 8-, 12-, and 16-foot lengths.

Logging residues. The unused portion of trees cut or destroyed during logging operations.

Merchantable portion. That portion of live trees 5.0 inches d.b.h. and larger between a 1-foot stump and a minimum 4.0-inch top d.o.b. on the central stem. That portion of primary forks from the point of occurrence to a minimum 4.0-inch top d.o.b. is included.

Merchantable volume. Solid-wood volume in the merchantable portion of live trees.

Noncommercial species. Tree species of typically small size, poor form, or inferior quality that normally do not develop into trees suitable for industrial wood products.

Nonforest land. Land that has never supported forests and land formerly forested where timber production is precluded by development for other uses.

Nongrowing-stock sources. The net volume removed from the nongrowing-stock portions of poletimber and sawtimber trees (stumps, tops, limbs, cull sections of central stem) and from any portion of a rough, rotten, sapling, dead, or nonforest tree.

Other forest land. Forest land other than timberland and productive reserved forest land. It includes available and reserved forest land that is incapable of producing annually 20 cubic feet per acre of industrial wood under natural conditions because of adverse site conditions such as sterile soils, dry climate, poor drainage, high elevation, steepness, or rockiness.

Other products. A miscellaneous category of roundwood products, e.g., cooperage, excelsior, shingles, and mill residue byproducts (charcoal, bedding, mulch, etc.).

Other removals. The growing-stock volume of trees removed from the inventory by cultural operations such as timber stand improvement, land clearing, and other changes in land use, resulting in the removal of the trees from timberland.

Other sources. (See: Nongrowing-stock sources.)

Ownership. The property owned by one ownership unit, including all parcels of land in the United States.

National forest land. Federal land that has been legally designated as national forests or purchase units, and other land under the administration of the Forest Service, including experimental areas and Bankhead-Jones Title III land.

Forest industry land. Land owned by companies or individuals operating primary wood-using plants.

Nonindustrial private forest (NIPF) land. Privately owned land excluding forest industry land.

Corporate. Owned by corporations, including incorporated farm ownerships.

Individual. All lands owned by individuals, including farm operators.

Other public. An ownership class that includes all public lands except national forests.

Miscellaneous Federal land. Federal land other than national forests.

State, county, and municipal land. Land owned by States, counties, and local public agencies or municipalities, or land leased to these governmental units for 50 years or more.

Plant residues. Wood material generated in the production of timber products at primary manufacturing plants.

Coarse residues. Material, such as slabs, edgings, trim, veneer cores and ends, which is suitable for chipping.

Fine residues. Material, such as sawdust, shavings, and veneer residue, which is not suitable for chipping.

Plant byproducts. Residues (coarse or fine) used in the further manufacture of industrial products for consumer use, or as fuel.

Unused plant residues. Residues (coarse or fine) that are not used for any product, including fuel.

Poletimber-size trees. Softwoods 5.0 to 8.9 inches d.b.h. and hardwoods 5.0 to 10.9 inches d.b.h.

Posts, poles, and pilings. Roundwood products milled (cut or peeled) into standard sizes (lengths and circumferences) to be put in the ground to provide vertical and lateral support in buildings, foundations, utility lines, and fences. May also include nonindustrial (unmilled) products.

Primary wood-using plants. Industries that convert roundwood products (saw logs, veneer logs, pulpwood, etc.) into primary wood products, such as lumber, veneer or sheathing, wood pulp.

Production. The total volume of known roundwood harvested from land within a State, regardless of where it is consumed. Production is the sum of timber harvested and used within a State, and all roundwood exported to other States.

Pulpwood. A roundwood product that will be reduced to individual wood fibers by chemical or mechanical means. The fibers are used to make a broad generic group of pulp products that includes paper products, as well as fiberboard, insulating board, and paperboard.

Receipts. The quantity or volume of industrial roundwood received at a mill or by a group of mills in a State, regardless of the geographic source. Volume of roundwood receipts is equal to the volume of roundwood retained in a State plus roundwood imported from other States.

Residential fuelwood. The volume of roundwood harvested to produce heat for residential settings.

Retained. Roundwood volume harvested from and processed by mills within the same State.

Rotten trees. Live trees of commercial species not containing at least one 12-foot saw log, or two noncontiguous saw logs, each 8 feet or longer, now or prospectively, primarily because of rot or missing sections, and with less than one-third of the gross board-foot tree volume in sound material.

Rough trees. Live trees of commercial species not containing at least one 12-foot saw log, or two noncontiguous saw logs, each 8 feet or longer, now or prospectively, primarily because of roughness, poor form, splits, and cracks, and with less than one-third of the gross board-foot tree volume in sound material; and live trees of noncommercial species.

Roundwood (roundwood logs). Logs, bolts, or other round sections cut from trees for industrial manufacture or consumer uses.

Roundwood chipped. Any timber cut primarily for industrial manufacture, delivered to nonpulpmills, chipped, and then sold to pulpmills for use as fiber. Includes tops, jump sections, whole trees, and pulpwood sticks.

Roundwood product drain. That portion of total drain used for a product.

Roundwood products. Any primary product, such as lumber, veneer, composite panels, poles, pilings, pulp, or fuelwood that is produced from roundwood.

Salvable dead trees. Standing or downed dead trees that were formerly growing stock and considered merchantable. Trees must be at least 5.0 inches d.b.h. to qualify.

Saplings. Live trees 1.0 to 5.0 inches d.b.h.

Saw log. A roundwood product, usually 8 feet in length or longer, processed into a variety of sawn products such as lumber, cants, pallets, railroad ties, and timbers.

Saw-log portion. The part of the bole of sawtimber trees between a 1-foot stump and the saw-log top.

Saw-log top. The point on the bole of sawtimber trees above which a conventional saw log cannot be produced. The minimum saw-log top is 7.0 inches d.o.b. for softwoods and 9.0 inches d.o.b. for hardwoods for FIA standards.

Sawtimber-size trees. Softwoods 9.0 inches d.b.h. and larger and hardwoods 11.0 inches d.b.h. and larger.

Sawtimber volume. Growing-stock volume in the saw-log portion of sawtimber-sized trees in board feet (International ¼-inch rule).

Seedlings. Trees < 1.0 inch d.b.h. and > 1 foot tall for hardwoods, > 6 inches tall for softwoods, and > 0.5 inch in diameter at ground level for longleaf pine.

Select red oaks. A group of several red oak species composed of cherrybark, Shumard, and northern red oaks. Other red oak species are included in the "other red oaks" group.

Select white oaks. A group of several white oak species composed of white, swamp chestnut, swamp white, chinkapin, Durand, and bur oaks. Other white oak species are included in the "other white oaks" group.

Softwoods. Coniferous trees, usually evergreen, having leaves that are needles or scale like.

Standard cord. A unit of measure applied to roundwood, usually bolts or split wood. It is a stack of wood 4 feet high, 4 feet wide, and 8 feet long encompassing 128 cubic feet of wood, bark, and air space. This usually translates to approximately 75.0 to 81.0 cubic feet of solid wood for pulpwood, because pulpwood is more uniform.

Standard unit. A unit measure applied to roundwood timber products. Board feet (International ¼-inch rule) is the standard unit used for saw logs and veneer; cords are used for pulpwood, composite panel, and fuelwood; hundred pieces for poles; thousand pieces for posts; and thousand cubic feet for all other miscellaneous forest products.

Timberland. Forest land capable of producing 20 cubic feet of industrial wood per acre per year and not withdrawn from timber utilization.

Timber product output. The total volume of roundwood products from all sources plus the volume of byproducts recovered from mill residues (equals roundwood product drain).

Timber products. Roundwood products and byproducts.

Timber removals. The total volume of trees removed from the timberland inventory by harvesting, cultural operations such as stand improvement, land clearing, or changes in land use. (Note: Includes roundwood products, logging residues, and other removals.)

Tree. Woody plants having one erect perennial stem or trunk at least 3 inches d.b.h., a more or less definitely formed crown of foliage, and a height of at least 13 feet (at maturity).

Upper-stem portion. The part of the main stem of sawtimber trees above the saw-log top and the minimum top diameter of 4.0 inches outside bark, or to the point where the main stem breaks into limbs.

Utilization studies. Studies conducted on active logging operations to develop factors for merchantable portions of trees left in the woods (logging residues), logging damage, and utilization of the unmerchantable portion of growing-stock trees and nongrowing-stock trees.

Veneer log. A roundwood product either rotary cut, sliced, stamped, or sawn into a variety of veneer products such as plywood, finished panels, veneer sheets, or sheathing.

Weight. A unit of measure for mill residues, expressed as oven-dry tons (2,000 oven-dry pounds).

Conversion Factors[a]

Saw logs	
Softwood	0.18018 cubic foot = 1 board foot
	5.55 board feet = 1 cubic foot
Hardwood	0.16556 cubic foot = 1 board foot
	6.04 board feet = 1 cubic foot
Veneer logs	
Softwood	0.17391 cubic foot = 1 board foot
	5.75 board feet = 1 cubic foot
Hardwood	0.15873 cubic foot = 1 board foot
	6.30 board feet = 1 cubic foot
Pulpwood[b]	
Softwood	72.5 cubic feet per cord
Hardwood	76.6 cubic feet per cord

[a] Conversion factors vary with stem size (d.b.h.) and species. The factors shown are for trees of average diameters removed in Arkansas during the most recent survey period.
[b] Cubic feet of solid wood per cord.

Species List[a]

Common name	Scientific name[b]	Common name	Scientific name[b]
Softwoods		**Hardwoods (continued)**	
Eastern redcedar	*Juniperus virginiana* L.	Apple	*Malus* spp. Mill.
Shortleaf pine	*Pinus echinata* Mill.	Chinaberry	*Melia azedarach* L.
Loblolly pine	*P. taeda* L.	White mulberry	*Morus alba* L.
Baldcypress	*Taxodium distichum* L.	Red mulberry	*M. rubra* L.
		Water tupelo	*Nyssa aquatica* L.
Hardwoods		Blackgum	*N. sylvatica* Marsh.
Florida maple	*Acer barbatum* Michx.	Swamp tupelo	*N. sylvatica* var. *biflora* (Walt.) Sarg.
Boxelder	*A. negundo* L.	Eastern hophornbeam	*Ostrya virginiana* (Mill.) K. Koch
Red maple	*A. rubrum* L.	Sourwood	*Oxydendrum arboreum* (L.) DC.
Silver maple	*A. saccharinum* L.	Royal paulownia	*Paulownia tomentosa* (Thunb.) Sieb.
Sugar maple	*A. saccharum* Marsh.		& Zucc. ex Steud.
Ohio buckeye	*Aesculus glabra* Willd.	Redbay	*Persea borbonia* (L.) Spreng.
Ailanthus	*Ailanthus altissima* (Mill.) Swingle	Water-elm	*Planera aquatica* J. F. Gmel.
Tung-oil-tree	*Aleurites fordii* Hemsl.	American sycamore	*Platanus occidentalis* L.
Serviceberry	*Amelanchier* spp. Medic.	Eastern cottonwood	*Populus deltoides* Bartr. ex Marsh.
River birch	*Betula nigra* L.	Plums, cherries (other than black cherry)	*Prunus* spp. L.
Chittamwood	*Bumelia lanuginosa* (Michx.) Pers.		
Water hickory	*Carya aquatica* (Michx. f.) Nutt.	Black cherry	*P. serotina* Ehrh.
Bitternut hickory	*C. cordiformis* (Wangenh.) K. Koch	White oak	*Quercus alba* L.
Pignut hickory	*C. glabra* (Mill.) Sweet	Scarlet oak	*Q. coccinea* Muenchh.
Pecan	*C. illinoensis* (Wangenh.) K. Koch	Durand oak	*Q. durandii* Buckl.
Shellbark hickory	*C. laciniosa* (Michx. f.) Loud.	Southern red oak	*Q. falcata* Michx.
Nutmeg hickory	*C. myristiciformis* (Michx. f.) Nutt.	Cherrybark oak	*Q. falcata* var. *pagodifolia* Ell.
Shagbark hickory	*C. ovata* (Mill.) K. Koch	Laurel oak	*Q. laurifolia* Michx.
Mockernut hickory	*C. tomentosa* (Poir.) Nutt.	Overcup oak	*Q. lyrata* Walt.
Allegheny chinkapin	*Castanea pumila* Mill.	Bur oak	*Q. macrocarpa* Michx.
Chinkapin	*Castanopsis* (D. Don) Spach	Blackjack oak	*Q. marilandica* Muenchh.
Sugarberry	*Celtis laevigata* Willd.	Swamp chestnut oak	*Q. michauxii* Nutt.
Hackberry	*C. occidentalis* L.	Chinkapin oak	*Q. muehlenbergii* Engelm.
Eastern redbud	*Cercis canadensis* L.	Water oak	*Q. nigra* L.
Flowering dogwood	*Cornus florida* L.	Nuttall oak	*Q. nuttallii* Palmer
American smoketree	*Cotinus obovatus* Raf.	Pin oak	*Q. palustris* Muenchh.
Hawthorn	*Crataegus* spp. L.	Willow oak	*Q. phellos* L.
Common persimmon	*Diospyros virginiana* L.	Northern red oak	*Q. rubra* L.
American beech	*Fagus grandifolia* Ehrh.	Shumard oak	*Q. shumardii* Buckl.
White ash	*Fraxinus americana* L.	Post oak	*Q. stellata* Wangenh.
Green ash	*F. pennsylvanica* Marsh.	Delta post oak	*Q. stellata* var. *paludosa* Sarg.
Pumpkin ash	*F. profunda* (Bush) Bush	Black oak	*Q. velutina* Lam.
Blue ash	*F. quadrangulata* Michx.	Black locust	*Robinia pseudoacacia* L.
Waterlocust	*Gleditsia aquatica* Marsh.	Willow	*Salix* spp. L.
Honeylocust	*G. triacanthos* L.	Sassafras	*Sassafras albidum* (Nutt.) Nees
Kentucky coffeetree	*Gymnocladus dioicus* (L.) K. Koch	American basswood	*Tilia americana* L.
American holly	*Ilex opaca* Ait.	White basswood	*T. heterophylla* Vent.
Butternut	*Juglans cinerea* L.	Winged elm	*Ulmus alata* Michx.
Black walnut	*J. nigra* L.	American elm	*U. americana* L.
Sweetgum	*Liquidambar styraciflua* L.	Cedar elm	*U. crassifolia* Nutt.
Yellow-poplar	*Liriodendron tulipifera* L.	Slippery elm	*U. rubra* Muhl.
Osage-orange	*Maclura pomifera* (Raf.) Schneid.	September elm	*U. serotina* Sarg.
Cucumbertree	*Magnolia acuminata* L.	Rock elm	*U. thomasii* Sarg.
Bigleaf magnolia	*M. macrophylla* Michx.	Sparkleberry	*Vaccinium arboreum* Marsh.
Sweetbay	*M. virginiana* L.		

[a] Common and scientific names of tree species >1.0 inch d.b.h. occurring in the FIA sample.
[b] Little (1979).

Appendix

Index of Tables

Table A.1—Output of industrial products by product and species group, Arkansas, 2007 and 2009

Product and species group	Year		Change	Change
	2007	2009		
	- - - - - thousand cubic feet - - - - -			*percent*
Saw logs				
Softwood	257,812	169,755	-88,057	-34.2
Hardwood	95,700	45,456	-50,244	-52.5
Total	353,512	215,211	-138,301	-39.1
Veneer logs				
Softwood	56,095	43,333	-12,762	-22.8
Hardwood	5,283	951	-4,332	-82.0
Total	61,378	44,284	-17,094	-27.9
Pulpwood[a]				
Softwood	135,715	133,200	-2,515	-1.9
Hardwood	94,061	81,285	-12,776	-13.6
Total	229,776	214,485	-15,291	-6.7
Composite panels				
Softwood	24,760	14,260	-10,500	-42.4
Hardwood	0	0	0	0
Total	24,760	14,260	-10,500	-42.4
Other industrial				
Softwood	331	1,193	862	260.4
Hardwood	2	0	-2	100.0
Total	333	1,193	860	258.3
All industrial				
Softwood	474,713	361,741	-112,972	-23.8
Hardwood	195,046	127,692	-67,354	-34.5
Total	669,759	489,433	-180,326	-26.9

[a] Includes roundwood delivered to nonpulpmills, then chipped and sold to pulpmills (2,170,000 cubic feet in 2007 and 742,000 cubic feet in 2009).

Table A.2—Roundwood receipts by product and species group, Arkansas, 2007 and 2009

Product and species group	Year			
	2007	2009	Change	Change
	- - - - - thousand cubic feet - - - - -			*percent*
Saw logs				
Softwood	293,004	188,237	-104,767	-35.8
Hardwood	95,582	42,956	-52,626	-55.1
Total	388,586	231,193	-157,393	-40.5
Veneer logs				
Softwood	68,796	52,354	-16,442	-23.9
Hardwood	6,543	951	-5,592	-85.5
Total	75,339	53,305	-22,034	-29.2
Pulpwood[a]				
Softwood	107,329	116,651	9,322	8.7
Hardwood	134,648	131,920	-2,728	-2.0
Total	241,977	248,571	6,594	2.7
Other industrial				
Softwood	22,235	14,393	-7,842	-35.3
Hardwood	0	0	0	0
Total	22,235	14,393	-7,842	-35.3
Total output				
Softwood	491,364	371,635	-119,729	-24.4
Hardwood	236,773	175,827	-60,946	-25.7
Total	728,137	547,462	-180,675	-24.8

[a] Includes roundwood delivered to nonpulpmills, then chipped and sold to pulpmills (2,459,000 cubic feet in 2007 and 832,000 cubic feet in 2009).

Table A.3—Number of primary wood-using plants by type of mill, Arkansas, 1968 to 2009

Type of mill	Year									
	1968	1971	1977	1987	1996	1999	2002	2005	2007	2009
	number									
Sawmills	448	278	384	274	286	308	260	139	127	75
Veneer or plywood mills	12	13	8	8	10	10	10	9	7	5
Pulpmills	7	7	8	8	8	8	6	6	6	6
Composite panel mills	0	0	0	0	0	0	1	1	1	1
Other mills	104	108	72	35	15	10	11	1	0	3
All plants	571	406	472	325	319	336	288	156	141	90

Table A.4—Roundwood receipts by sawmill size, Arkansas, 2007 and 2009

Sawmill size class[a]	2007			2009		
	Mills	Volume		Mills	Volume	
mmbf	number	mbf	percent	number	mbf	percent
<1	5	1,433	0	5	920	0
1.0–4.99	55	167,550	8	38	109,229	9
5.0–9.99	32	210,865	10	10	65,531	5
10.0–49.99	22	427,850	19	12	304,467	23
>50	13	1,396,033	63	10	824,641	63
Total	127	2,203,731	100	75	1,304,788	100

[a] Based on volume received as opposed to actual capacity.

Table A.5—Roundwood receipts by species and type of mill, Arkansas, 2009

Species	All mills	Sawmills	Type of mill		Pulpmills[a]	Other mills
			Veneer mills			
			Pine plywood	Other veneer		
			thousand cubic feet			
Softwood						
Yellow pine	254,904	188,181	52,354	0	NA	14,369
Eastern white pine	0	0	0	0	NA	0
Cedar	52	28	0	0	NA	24
Cypress	10	10	0	0	NA	0
Other softwood	18	18	0	0	NA	0
Unclassified	116,651	0	0	0	116,651	0
Total softwoods	371,635	188,237	52,354	0	116,651	14,393
Hardwood						
Blackgum and tupelo	1,115	925	0	190	NA	0
Soft maple	126	126	0	0	NA	0
Sweetgum	3,378	3,092	0	286	NA	0
Yellow-poplar	1,394	1,394	0	0	NA	0
Other soft hardwood	1,892	1,417	0	475	NA	0
Hickory	2,837	2,837	0	0	NA	0
Red oak	18,470	18,470	0	0	NA	0
White oak	11,292	11,292	0	0	NA	0
Other hard hardwood	3,403	3,403	0	0	NA	0
Unclassified	131,920	0	0	0	131,920	0
Total hardwoods	175,827	42,956	0	951	131,920	0
All species	547,462	231,193	52,354	951	248,571	14,393

NA = not applicable.

[a] Collected only by softwood and hardwood and includes roundwood chipped.

Table A.6—Industrial roundwood movement by year and species group, Arkansas, 2007 and 2009

Year	Production	Exported to other States	Retained	Imported from other States	Receipts
			thousand cubic feet		
		Softwood			
2007	474,713	59,125	415,588	75,776	491,364
2009	361,741	36,753	324,988	46,647	371,635
		Hardwood			
2007	195,046	24,710	170,336	66,437	236,773
2009	127,692	12,585	115,107	60,720	175,827
		All species			
2007	669,759	83,835	585,924	142,213	728,137
2009	489,433	49,338	440,095	107,367	547,462

Table A.7—Industrial roundwood movement by product and species group, Arkansas, 2009

Product and species group	Production	Exported to other States	Retained	Imported from other States	Receipts
			thousand cubic feet		
Saw logs					
Softwood	169,755	3,706	166,049	22,188	188,237
Hardwood	45,456	4,518	40,938	2,018	42,956
Total	215,211	8,224	206,987	24,206	231,193
Veneer logs					
Softwood	43,333	0	43,333	9,021	52,354
Hardwood	951	0	951	0	951
Total	44,284	0	44,284	9,021	53,305
Pulpwood[a]					
Softwood	133,200	31,987	101,213	15,438	116,651
Hardwood	81,285	8,067	73,218	58,702	131,920
Total	214,485	40,054	174,431	74,140	248,571
Other industrial					
Softwood	15,453	1,060	14,393	0	14,393
Hardwood	0	0	0	0	0
Total	15,453	1,060	14,393	0	14,393
All products					
Softwood	361,741	36,753	324,988	46,647	371,635
Hardwood	127,692	12,585	115,107	60,720	175,827
Total	489,433	49,338	440,095	107,367	547,462

[a] Includes roundwood chipped.

Table A.8—Saw-log volume by destination, source, and species group, Arkansas, 2009

Destination and source	All species	Species group	
		Softwood	Hardwood
		thousand cubic feet	
Arkansas (retained)	206,987	166,049	40,938
Exports to			
Louisiana	444	0	444
Missouri	3,386	67	3,319
Oklahoma	2,003	1,356	647
Tennessee	59	43	16
Texas	2,332	2,240	92
Total	8,224	3,706	4,518
Imports from			
Louisiana	17,498	16,070	1,428
Missouri	438	438	0
Oklahoma	6,270	5,680	590
Total	24,206	22,188	2,018

Table A.10—Pulpwood volume by destination, source, and species group, Arkansas, 2009[a]

Destination and source	All species	Species group	
		Softwood	Hardwood
		thousand cubic feet	
Arkansas (retained)	174,431	101,213	73,218
Exports to			
Kentucky	176	0	176
Louisiana	14,476	14,475	1
Oklahoma	12,487	12,268	219
Texas	12,915	5,244	7,671
Total	40,054	31,987	8,067
Imports from			
Louisiana	21,657	5,734	15,923
Mississippi	16,564	992	15,572
Missouri	18	16	2
Oklahoma	9,496	1,598	7,898
Tennessee	27	0	27
Texas	26,378	7,098	19,280
Total	74,140	15,438	58,702

[a] Includes roundwood delivered to nonpulpmills, then chipped and sold to pulpmills.

Table A.9—Veneer volume by destination, source, and species group, Arkansas, 2009

Destination and source	All species	Species group	
		Softwood	Hardwood
		thousand cubic feet	
Arkansas (retained)	44,284	43,333	951
Imports from			
Louisiana	9,021	9,021	0
Total	9,021	9,021	0

Table A.11—Other industrial volume by destination, source, and species group, Arkansas, 2009[a]

Destination and source	All species	Species group	
		Softwood	Hardwood
		thousand cubic feet	
Arkansas (retained)	14,393	14,393	0
Exports to			
Louisiana	103	103	0
Mississippi	281	281	0
Missouri	96	96	0
Oklahoma	544	544	0
Texas	36	36	0
Total	1,060	1,060	0

[a] Includes poles, posts, mulch, composite panels, firewood, log homes, charcoal, and all other industrial mills.

Table A.12—Primary mill residue volume by roundwood type, species group, and residue type, Arkansas, 2009

Roundwood type and species group	All types	Residue type			
		Bark	Coarse	Sawdust	Shavings
		thousand cubic feet			
Saw logs					
Softwood	117,376	12,637	54,343	33,385	17,011
Hardwood	27,569	4,455	13,737	8,649	728
Total	144,945	17,092	68,080	42,034	17,739
Veneer logs					
Softwood	21,144	3,636	11,484	6,024	0
Hardwood	354	103	166	85	0
Total	21,498	3,739	11,650	6,109	0
Pulpwood					
Softwood	11,959	11,959	0	0	0
Hardwood	16,692	16,692	0	0	0
Total	28,651	28,651	0	0	0
Other industrial[a]					
Softwood	1,604	1,521	83	0	0
Hardwood	0	0	0	0	0
Total	1,604	1,521	83	0	0
Total					
Softwood	152,083	29,753	65,910	39,409	17,011
Hardwood	44,615	21,250	13,903	8,734	728
Total	196,698	51,003	79,813	48,143	17,739

[a] Includes poles, pilings, posts, composite panels and other industrial products.

Table A.13—Disposal of residue at primary wood-using plants by product, species group, and type of residue, Arkansas, 2007 and 2009

Product and species group	All types		Bark		Coarse		Sawdust		Shavings	
	2007	2009	2007	2009	2007	2009	2007	2009	2007	2009
					thousand cubic feet					
Fiber products										
Softwood	96,308	64,685	0	0	92,503	64,685	2,247	0	1,558	0
Hardwood	19,560	8,654	0	0	19,560	8,654	0	0	0	0
Total	115,868	73,339	0	0	112,063	73,339	2,247	0	1,558	0
Particleboard										
Softwood	15,022	7,762	0	0	455	706	547	1,943	14,020	5,113
Hardwood	0	0	0	0	0	0	0	0	0	0
Total	15,022	7,762	0	0	455	706	547	1,943	14,020	5,113
Charcoal/ chemical wood										
Softwood	0	0	0	0	0	0	0	0	0	0
Hardwood	1,119	998	112	104	651	593	356	301	0	0
Total	1,119	998	112	104	651	593	356	301	0	0
Sawn products										
Softwood	0	0	0	0	0	0	0	0	0	0
Hardwood	0	0	0	0	0	0	0	0	0	0
Total	0	0	0	0	0	0	0	0	0	0
Industrial fuel										
Softwood	101,234	77,874	37,294	28,364	1,413	416	55,843	37,395	6,684	11,699
Hardwood	56,479	33,046	25,700	19,811	10,664	4,452	18,351	8,079	1,764	704
Total	157,713	110,920	62,994	48,175	12,077	4,868	74,194	45,474	8,448	12,403
Miscellaneous										
Softwood	6,912	1,732	1,690	1,385	87	87	1,240	61	3,895	199
Hardwood	3,056	1,729	1,625	1,305	513	104	833	296	85	24
Total	9,968	3,461	3,315	2,690	600	191	2,073	357	3,980	223
Not used										
Softwood	2	30	2	4	0	16	0	10	0	0
Hardwood	972	188	201	30	487	100	284	58	0	0
Total	974	218	203	34	487	116	284	68	0	0
All products										
Softwood	219,478	152,083	38,986	29,753	94,458	65,910	59,877	39,409	26,157	17,011
Hardwood	81,186	44,615	27,638	21,250	31,875	13,903	19,824	8,734	1,849	728
Total	300,664	196,698	66,624	51,003	126,333	79,813	79,701	48,143	28,006	17,739

Table A.14—Roundwood timber product output by county, product, and species group, Arkansas, 2009

County	All products Soft-wood	All products Hard-wood	Saw logs Soft-wood	Saw logs Hard-wood	Veneer logs Soft-wood	Veneer logs Hard-wood	Pulpwood[a] Soft-wood	Pulpwood[a] Hard-wood	Composite panels Soft-wood	Composite panels Hard-wood	Other industrial Soft-wood	Other industrial Hard-wood
						thousand cubic feet						
Arkansas	292	1,376	0	355	0	190	292	831	0	0	0	0
Ashley	21,593	8,810	4,084	635	8,958	0	8,453	8,175	0	0	98	0
Baxter	201	408	28	97	0	0	77	311	0	0	96	0
Benton	0	840	0	840	0	0	0	0	0	0	0	0
Boone	67	436	64	352	0	0	3	84	0	0	0	0
Bradley	28,334	3,558	7,948	129	5,996	0	11,066	3,429	3,268	0	56	0
Calhoun	12,882	2,537	5,091	1,121	2,278	0	2,381	1,416	3,132	0	0	0
Carroll	9	651	9	651	0	0	0	0	0	0	0	0
Chicot	75	810	0	0	0	0	75	810	0	0	0	0
Clark	13,266	10,843	6,148	3,391	3,076	0	3,681	7,452	272	0	89	0
Clay	0	591	0	591	0	0	0	0	0	0	0	0
Cleburne	4,163	819	2,376	285	0	0	1,787	534	0	0	0	0
Cleveland	16,777	3,236	8,323	920	1,398	0	5,460	2,316	1,498	0	98	0
Columbia	6,108	3,397	4,469	1,557	142	0	1,394	1,840	103	0	0	0
Conway	4,120	382	2,606	0	0	0	1,514	382	0	0	0	0
Craighead	67	34	66	34	0	0	1	0	0	0	0	0
Crawford	0	584	0	584	0	0	0	0	0	0	0	0
Crittenden	44	46	43	0	0	0	1	46	0	0	0	0
Cross	0	116	0	77	0	0	0	39	0	0	0	0
Dallas	19,849	3,892	7,610	1,142	4,216	0	5,906	2,750	2,042	0	75	0
Desha	132	1,904	0	0	0	0	132	1,904	0	0	0	0
Drew	19,472	2,127	4,209	276	3,736	0	11,227	1,851	272	0	28	0
Faulkner	1,219	334	518	0	0	190	701	144	0	0	0	0
Franklin	763	233	634	150	0	0	129	83	0	0	0	0
Fulton	0	2,310	0	2,310	0	0	0	0	0	0	0	0
Garland	8,344	590	6,276	329	485	0	1,583	261	0	0	0	0
Grant	13,518	2,212	6,476	601	1,433	0	4,384	1,611	1,225	0	0	0
Greene	78	21	4	21	0	0	74	0	0	0	0	0
Hempstead	6,276	2,383	2,733	220	1,295	0	2,181	2,163	0	0	67	0
Hot Spring	9,388	1,860	4,051	1,031	1,233	0	3,614	829	408	0	82	0
Howard	11,067	2,706	5,827	392	162	0	5,027	2,314	0	0	51	0
Independence	1,106	2,677	241	506	0	0	865	2,171	0	0	0	0
Izard	1,561	486	1,450	414	0	0	111	72	0	0	0	0
Jackson	0	172	0	162	0	0	0	10	0	0	0	0
Jefferson	4,876	1,567	905	694	199	0	3,500	873	272	0	0	0
Johnson	1,539	1,712	867	74	0	0	672	1,638	0	0	0	0
Lafayette	2,632	2,234	969	852	0	0	1,663	1,382	0	0	0	0
Lawrence	22	835	2	661	0	0	20	174	0	0	0	0
Lee	0	354	0	117	0	0	0	237	0	0	0	0
Lincoln	4,496	2,981	2,207	171	799	0	1,354	2,810	136	0	0	0
Little River	3,788	3,812	1,131	647	0	0	2,412	3,165	185	0	60	0
Logan	4,788	481	4,233	74	0	0	531	407	0	0	24	0
Lonoke	253	942	66	724	0	143	187	75	0	0	0	0
Madison	0	2,507	0	2,265	0	0	0	242	0	0	0	0
Marion	158	549	139	391	0	0	19	158	0	0	0	0
Miller	3,346	1,419	2,605	401	0	0	705	1,018	0	0	36	0
Mississippi	0	89	0	89	0	0	0	0	0	0	0	0

continued

Table A.14—Roundwood timber product output by county, product, and species group, Arkansas, 2009 (continued)

County	All products		Saw logs		Veneer logs		Pulpwood[a]		Composite panels		Other industrial	
	Soft-wood	Hard-wood	Soft-wood	Hard-wood	Soft-wood	Hard-wood	Soft-wood	Hard-wood	Soft-wood	Hard-wood	Soft-wood	Hard-wood
	thousand cubic feet											
Monroe	14	721	0	499	0	0	14	222	0	0	0	0
Montgomery	2,429	1,806	1,887	1,440	0	0	491	366	0	0	51	0
Nevada	9,554	2,004	4,833	987	2,429	0	2,225	1,017	0	0	67	0
Newton	771	868	741	781	0	0	30	87	0	0	0	0
Ouachita	8,775	5,077	5,060	2,883	647	0	2,251	2,194	817	0	0	0
Perry	10,581	434	7,102	65	0	0	3,479	369	0	0	0	0
Phillips	62	624	0	117	0	0	62	507	0	0	0	0
Pike	21,125	3,012	10,293	1,403	3,238	0	7,505	1,609	0	0	89	0
Poinsett	6	32	3	32	0	0	3	0	0	0	0	0
Polk	11,185	2,170	7,064	1,065	0	0	3,891	1,105	179	0	51	0
Pope	4,305	1,206	3,558	186	0	0	732	1,020	0	0	15	0
Prairie	242	821	0	515	0	0	242	306	0	0	0	0
Pulaski	1,931	855	1,202	211	0	238	729	406	0	0	0	0
Randolph	0	1,158	0	1,156	0	0	0	2	0	0	0	0
St. Francis	30	454	0	17	0	0	30	437	0	0	0	0
Saline	8,211	1,322	4,051	402	809	95	3,215	825	136	0	0	0
Scott	5,538	1,694	3,144	518	0	0	2,394	1,176	0	0	0	0
Searcy	1,067	1,207	798	413	0	0	269	794	0	0	0	0
Sebastian	402	0	0	0	0	0	402	0	0	0	0	0
Sevier	7,455	2,093	3,531	250	0	0	3,685	1,843	179	0	60	0
Sharp	288	769	1	549	0	0	287	220	0	0	0	0
Stone	836	1,619	239	932	0	0	597	687	0	0	0	0
Union	22,923	5,489	13,257	1,284	804	0	8,726	4,205	136	0	0	0
Van Buren	3,997	3,504	1,817	159	0	0	2,180	3,345	0	0	0	0
Washington	0	1,387	0	1,375	0	0	0	12	0	0	0	0
White	4,568	2,189	462	1,284	0	95	4,106	810	0	0	0	0
Woodruff	45	649	0	600	0	0	45	49	0	0	0	0
Yell	8,732	1,665	6,304	0	0	0	2,428	1,665	0	0	0	0
All counties	361,741	127,692	169,755	45,456	43,333	951	133,200	81,285	14,260	0	1,193	0

[a] Includes roundwood delivered to nonpulpmills, then chipped and sold to pulpmills (742,000 cubic feet in 2009).

Table A.15—Total roundwood output by product, species group, and source of material, Arkansas, 2009

| Product and species group | All sources | Total | Growing-stock trees | | Other sources |
			Sawtimber	Poletimber	
			thousand cubic feet		
Saw logs					
Softwood	169,755	165,640	155,702	9,938	4,115
Hardwood	45,456	44,392	41,750	2,641	1,064
Total	215,211	210,032	197,452	12,579	5,179
Veneer logs and bolts					
Softwood	43,333	42,249	40,560	1,690	1,084
Hardwood	951	934	934	0	17
Total	44,284	43,184	41,494	1,690	1,100
Pulpwood					
Softwood	133,200	124,717	72,512	52,205	8,483
Hardwood	81,285	77,009	38,743	38,266	4,276
Total	214,485	201,726	111,255	90,471	12,759
Composite panels					
Softwood	14,260	12,152	6,249	5,903	2,108
Hardwood	0	0	0	0	0
Total	14,260	12,152	6,249	5,903	2,108
Poles and posts					
Softwood	1,063	873	797	75	190
Hardwood	0	0	0	0	0
Total	1,063	873	797	75	190
Other miscellaneous					
Softwood	130	123	97	26	7
Hardwood	0	0	0	0	0
Total	130	123	97	26	7
Total industrial products					
Softwood	361,741	345,754	275,917	69,837	15,987
Hardwood	127,692	122,335	81,428	40,907	5,357
Total	489,433	468,089	357,345	110,745	21,344
Residential fuelwood					
Softwood	2,807	2,442	1,956	486	365
Hardwood	22,478	18,825	16,025	2,799	3,653
Total	25,285	21,266	17,981	3,285	4,019
All products					
Softwood	364,548	348,196	277,873	70,323	16,352
Hardwood	150,170	141,160	97,453	43,707	9,010
Total	514,718	489,356	375,326	114,030	25,362

Numbers in rows and columns may not sum to totals due to rounding.

Table A.16—Total roundwood output by species group, survey region, and ownership class, Arkansas, 2009

Species group and survey region	Total	Ownership class		
		Public	Forest industry	Nonindustrial private
		thousand cubic feet		
Softwoods				
South Delta	10,523	10	6,032	4,481
North Delta	294	0	2	292
Southwest	260,132	3,543	159,970	96,619
Ouachita	62,624	19,465	27,907	15,252
Ozark	30,975	1,063	6,661	23,251
Total softwoods	364,548	24,081	200,572	139,895
Hardwoods				
South Delta	14,231	1,697	3,887	8,647
North Delta	3,574	0	479	3,095
Southwest	85,497	1,094	29,818	54,585
Ouachita	12,957	6,044	1,386	5,527
Ozark	33,911	3,198	1,070	29,643
Total hardwoods	150,170	12,033	36,640	101,497
All species	514,718	36,114	237,212	241,392

Numbers in rows and columns may not sum to totals due to rounding.

Table A.17—Total roundwood output by species group, detailed species group, and product, Arkansas, 2009

Species group and detailed species group	Total	Saw logs	Veneer logs	Pulpwood	Composite panels	Poles and posts	Other miscellaneous	Residential fuelwood
				thousand cubic feet				
Softwood								
Cedar	4,203	2,394	1	1,767	4	1	4	32
Loblolly-shortleaf pine	358,543	166,789	43,159	130,400	14,247	1,060	126	2,762
Other yellow pines	508	127	0	377	0	0	0	4
Cypress	1,294	445	173	655	9	2	0	10
Total softwoods	364,548	169,755	43,333	133,200	14,260	1,063	130	2,807
Hardwood								
Soft maple	2,157	694	6	1,134	0	0	0	323
Hard maple	349	273	0	24	0	0	0	52
Hickory	12,888	4,336	75	6,548	0	0	0	1,929
Beech	723	311	0	304	0	0	0	108
Ash	3,254	1,012	27	1,727	0	0	0	487
Black walnut	156	117		16	0	0	0	23
Sweetgum	24,967	5,877	117	15,236	0	0	0	3,737
Yellow-poplar	50	42	0	0	0	0	0	7
Blackgum-tupelo	4,076	1,253	4	2,209	0	0	0	610
Sycamore	762	253	5	390	0	0	0	114
Cottonwood	1,611	762	46	562	0	0	0	241
Black cherry	850	210	3	509	0	0	0	127
Select white oaks	20,657	6,789	123	10,653	0	0	0	3,092
Other white oaks	17,615	5,494	149	9,335	0	0	0	2,636
Select red oaks	10,216	3,131	10	5,546	0	0	0	1,529
Other red oaks	39,305	11,992	301	21,127	0	0	0	5,884
Basswood	35	29	0	0	0	0	0	5
Elm	4,210	1,239	38	2,303	0	0	0	630
Other eastern hardwoods	6,290	1,643	45	3,660	0	0	0	942
Total hardwoods	150,170	45,456	951	81,285	0	0	0	22,478
All species	514,718	215,211	44,284	214,485	14,260	1,063	130	25,285

Numbers in rows and columns may not sum to totals due to rounding.

Table A.18—Total roundwood output by species group, detailed species group, and ownership class, Arkansas, 2009

Species group and detailed species group	Total	Ownership class		
		Public	Forest industry	Nonindustrial private
		thousand cubic feet		
Softwood				
Cedar	4,203	90	297	3,816
Loblolly-shortleaf pine	358,543	23,966	199,614	134,963
Other yellow pines	508	0	2	506
Cypress	1,294	25	659	610
Total softwoods	364,548	24,081	200,572	139,895
Hardwood				
Soft maple	2,157	71	657	1,428
Hard maple	349	0	0	349
Hickory	12,888	963	2,410	9,515
Beech	723	27	179	517
Ash	3,254	306	818	2,130
Black walnut	156	0	0	156
Sweetgum	24,967	1,288	6,794	16,885
Yellow-poplar	50	0	0	50
Blackgum-tupelo	4,076	246	830	3,000
Sycamore	762	4	136	622
Cottonwood	1,611	176	68	1,367
Black cherry	850	60	109	681
Select white oaks	20,657	2,662	4,584	13,411
Other white oaks	17,615	2,057	4,385	11,173
Select red oaks	10,216	853	2,653	6,709
Other red oaks	39,305	2,364	10,219	26,721
Basswood	35	0	0	35
Elm	4,210	426	903	2,881
Other eastern hardwoods	6,290	530	1,894	3,866
Total hardwoods	150,170	12,033	36,640	101,497
All species	514,718	36,114	237,212	241,392

Numbers in rows and columns may not sum to totals due to rounding.

www.ingramcontent.com/pod-product-compliance
Lightning Source LLC
Chambersburg PA
CBHW081134280526

45787CB00007B/3077